Scruffy Little Essays

Scruffy Little Essays

A COLLECTION ON KNOX COUNTY 2007-08

David L. Page, Ph.D.

Warped Minds Press

Knoxville, Tennessee

Copyright © 2024 by David L. Page, Ph.D.

All rights reserved.

No portion of this book may be reproduced in any form without written permission from the publisher or author, except as permitted by U.S. copyright law.

This publication is designed to provide accurate and authoritative information in regard to the subject matter covered. It is sold with the understanding that neither the author nor the publisher is engaged in rendering legal, investment, accounting, or other professional services. While the publisher and author have used their best efforts in preparing this book, they make no representations or warranties with respect to the accuracy or completeness of the contents of this book and expressly disclaim any implied warranties of merchantability or fitness for a particular purpose. No warranty may be created or extended by sales representatives or written sales materials. The advice and strategies contained herein may not be suitable for your situation. You should consult with a professional when appropriate. Neither the publisher nor the author shall be liable for any loss of profit or any other commercial damages, including but not limited to special, incidental, consequential, personal, or other damages. For permission requests, write to the publisher, addressed "Attention: Permissions Coordinator," at the address below.

Warped Minds Press
8410 Corteland Drive
Knoxville, Tennessee 37909
www.warpedminds.io

Book Layout ©2017 BookDesignTemplates.com

Ordering Information:

Quantity sales. Special discounts are available on quantity purchases by corporations, associations, and others. Contact the "Special Sales Department" at the address above for details.

Scruffy Little Essays/David L. Page. Ph.D.—1st ed.

ISBN 979-8-9906504-5-9 (Paperback)
ISBN 979-8-9906504-6-6 (eBook)

Books also by David L. Page, PhD.

The Art of the Compromise
Returning American Democracy to Better Days

Knox County 2012 Charter Review Committee
Personal Notes and Position Papers

Just as all politics is local, all good history is personal.

—Marcia Clark
Lead prosecutor, 1994 OJ Simpson trial

Contents

Introduction 1
Ch. 1. Finding My Local Voice 11
Ch. 2. Noting Public Interests 19
Ch. 3. Observing Government 31
Ch. 4. Exploring Other Topics 41
Ch. 5. Digging into Politics 53
Ch. 6. Publishing the Unpublished 63
Conclusion 85
Acknowledgments 89
Work Cited 91

INTRODUCTION

Becoming a Writer

I HAVE OFTEN SAID that I hate writing and reading, but I love the results. Much like working out at the gym, no one enjoys the process as much as they enjoy the results. Such is my relationship with writing and reading. I thoroughly enjoy the results—the sharpness of my thoughts, the crispness of my ideas, the depths of my expression—but the process is arduous—stumbling through word choice, watching grammar, slogging through pronunciations. In the end, my mind is better for it, though.

This book represents a major step in my becoming a writer. The book is a collection of essays I wrote from 2007 to 2008 as a Community Columnist for the Knoxville News Sentinel. Before jumping into these opinion columns, I thought I would briefly introduce my path to becoming a writer. That path starts with becoming a reader first and progresses to becoming a writer. It's not a path I thought I would take, but it may be helpful to share. Writing the opinion columns pushed me into a realm beyond my academic publications and was an important step in my self-publishing journey.

However, my writing is not perfect, and I chose the title *Scruffy Little Essays* to reflect that imperfection. The title alludes to an insult by the Wall Street Journal in 1981 (Daniel, 1981) when Knoxville was preparing to host the 1982 World's Fair. The Journal was unimpressed with Knoxville and the city's efforts. The 1981 article ridiculed Knoxville as "a scruffy little city of 180,000 on the Tennessee Rivier." The Journal ran that dismissive quote under the headline "What If You Gave A World's Fair And Nobody Came?"

Ouch!

Knoxville has since turned that put-down into a badge of honor—as mountain folk are known to do. Since the caliber of my writing is questionable, I thought the "scruffy" label might also fit here. I've come to embrace the imperfections in my writing, and the 'scruffy' label is a reminder of that. It's a reflection of my journey as a writer, where I've learned to appreciate the rough edges and the beauty in imperfection.

Becoming a Reader

In high school, my family and I traveled to Thomas Jefferson's home, Monticello, in Charlottesville, Virginia. I was in awe. I fell in love with the mind and creativity of our nation's third president. Jefferson designed and built Monticello with unique and novel innovations behind each door. The roof collected water to supply the mountaintop home. A wall-sized clock used cannonballs to track days. A mechanical pen contraption followed his handwriting to create duplicates of his letters. Jefferson was a creative individual.

In the gift shop—all such homes end with a gift shop—a quote from Jefferson, hanging on a poster, caught my eye. "I cannot live without books." This strange phrase puzzled me. Jefferson preferred death without his books, and that phrase stuck with me.

I was never a reader in primary or secondary school, much less a writer. When I was younger, I struggled to read books for assigned book reports in school. I would read so far into the book, and then, in desperation, as assignment deadlines drew near, I would ask my mother to finish reading the book aloud to me. As a loving mother would do, she obliged and indulged me. Who could refuse reading to their child? I never picked up a book that I was not required to read except for a few odd computer manuals from time to time. I did not enjoy reading.

In college, a friend noted during a casual conversation that "all great leaders read." His comment was a throwaway one in a discussion that no one likely remembers except me. It stuck with me. It burrowed into my brain along with Jefferson's quote. I began paying attention to significant historical figures and their relationship to reading books. A light bulb went off. I noticed a strong correlation between renowned leaders in history, people who made an impact, and their intense consumption of books.

In my senior year in college, I made a decision. I would become a "reader." I committed to picking a book and reading it from front to back. I was a slow reader, so this task was not easy initially. But I was determined. Based on a recommendation, my first book was Tom Clancy's Hunt for Red October. And it was a revelation. I was hooked from the first page. The storyline and the technical details Clancy is famous for delivering kept me enthralled. I could not have picked a better book to start my journey. It took me almost three months to read that book, but I savored every page. And I soon read his follow-up books, including Patriot Games and Red Storm Rising. It was a joyous experience that marked the beginning of my love for reading.

My next big step happened during my first year of graduate school as a Masters student. I was visiting B. Dalton bookstore in the Fort Henry Mall while on holiday break in Kingsport, Tennessee. At the front of the store, a collection of biographies sat on a display table. As I browsed the table, I saw Saul Padover's Thomas Jefferson biography, an abridged version. I grabbed it and started my journey down a lifelong passion for nonfiction. I devoured Padover's book. When I returned to campus from the holiday break, I finished reading the book, marking and annotating passages, and dovetailing key pages.

I had become a reader. I now mostly read nonfiction books. My library has almost 1,000 books, and I would estimate that 90% are nonfiction. I am particularly drawn to biographies and historical nonfiction, as they allow me to delve into the lives and stories of remarkable individuals. The next step in my journey was to become a writer, too.

Expressing My Thoughts

My journey to become a writer was a slightly different path. Like reading, I also have struggled as a writer. My biggest hurdle is the mechanics of getting my thoughts down on paper. My thoughts are not fluid as my mind interrupts me to find the correct spelling, to form the proper punctuation, or to—well, many little interruptions intercept my primary thought before I can transfer it to paper. It's a struggle that many writers can relate to, and it's a part of my journey that I'm not afraid to share.

I have learned over the years that the interruptions are worse when I handwrite my thoughts. The delay in forming letters with a single hand is too slow, and my mind outpaces my hand. However, I have found that typing my thoughts shortcircuits these wandering interruptions and affords me the best opportunity to get my ideas down on paper. My ten fingers can keep up—at least to a manageable degree—with my thoughts. This skill developed in high school when I took typing classes and progressed more fully in graduate school when I wrote my Master's thesis.

Oddly, though, the foremost step in my writing ability occurred when I worked as a research engineer at the Naval Surface Warfare Center in

Dahlgren, Virginia. This job was my first work since graduating with my Master's degree. By luck, I started an email list to share life experiences with college friends who were now scattered at various jobs across the southeast. I began sharing stories about my life in Dahlgren through the email newsletter. I had never written stories for pleasure before, and somehow, without the pressure of a looming deadline or impending grade, my thoughts flowed more effortlessly from my mind to the page. I was writing! And I enjoyed it. I did not experience the constant interruptions of my mind complaining about spelling, syntax, and other flow-stopping interjections.

I learned something about myself in this freedom to write without judgment. In my early school years, I approached writing like one might about carving a wood sculpture or a marble statue. Each cut removes a piece that cannot be replaced, so choose and cut carefully. This approach to my ginger and trepid writing was slow to transfer my thoughts to words on paper. I was afraid to write. An alternative metaphor is a sculpture with clay that adds pieces, removes pieces, adds again, and continues adding, removing, molding, cutting, and sculpting a piece. No touch is final. No fear. Each movement of the clay is tentative and refinable. This insight changed my approach to writing. I have become a clay, rather than a stone, sculptor. When I write, my first goal is to get my thoughts out of my mind and onto paper with little care for their quality or structure. Then, I step back, take a break, and look at what I have. I then refine, rework, rewrite, and rebuild. I have found that I never reach a final version of a writing product, only the latest draft. I can continually refine and improve.

I had become a writer and a reader. While I'm not Jefferson or Shakespeare, I have learned that that combination is powerful. My creativity and insights into problems have expanded enormously. I can feel the difference in my mind. The arsenal of weapons that my brain has access to includes many thinkers, from Jefferson to Shakespeare, Doris Kearns Goodwin to Tom Clancy, Gordon Woods to Gerald Posner. I still do not enjoy reading and writing, but the results are worth it.

Yet, my reader-writer journey had more steps ahead.

Publishing to the World

In 1997, I left Dahlgren and returned to graduate school, this time to pursue a PhD at the University of Tennessee. Here, I would publish my ideas to the world for the first time, and I must confess that I loved it. I loved attacking a problem, finding a new insight, and then communicating that insight in a more digestible form to the world. My five years in the PhD program helped me hone my skills as a reader and writer. I still have the 15 boxes of academic papers I photocopied and read in preparation for my PhD defense. Many of those papers made it to the reference list of my dissertation.

My dissertation was another essential step in my writing career. I would write chapter after chapter, month after month, in my final year. I would carry drafts with me to read and edit. I would have a stack of papers at basketball games cheering on the Vols, at Denny's eating a greasy burger at 1:00 AM, and at the library double-checking citations. I learned the shared craft of reading to build arguments and writing to mesh my thoughts into those arguments. I learned the diligence of documenting sources to stand on the shoulders of giants. Again, I was no Albert Einstein, but I developed a passion for the process based on the results. In those results, I also found an outlet for my political thoughts.

Writing as a Community Columnist

When I graduated with my PhD, I carried this passion into my career and private life, where I dabbled in politics. I have been involved in politics since as early as I can remember. My uncle Lon V. Boyd was the County Executive for Sullivan County, where I grew up. Uncle Momo, as I affectionately knew him, campaigned throughout the county, and I have fond memories of helping him. We would hand out push cards, ride in parades, and attend barbeques.

One day, while reading the Knoxville News Sentinel, my wife Lisa read their call for budding opinion writers to submit article ideas for possible selection as Community Columnists. The contest would select authors based on their entries to write opinion columns to appear once a month in the

Sunday paper. Lisa encouraged me to try my hand. I submitted an entry and was selected.

The essays that follow are the columns that I wrote. My opinions expressed in these columns have sometimes grown more robust and, in other cases, have changed. They have evolved over the 15 years since I first wrote these columns. While I often hate the process of reading and writing, it is this process that is more important than the results. Like my opinions, the results may change, but I have learned that I must maintain the process—read, write, and repeat.

CHAPTER 1

Finding My Local Voice

BEING SELECTED TO WRITE as a Community Columnist for the Knoxville News Sentinel was a tremendous growth opportunity for me. I was intimidated as I did not consider myself a polished author. I had ideas that I wanted to share, but I had not shared them beyond a few close friends. The Sentinel platform was more than a few friends, with over 150,000 print subscribers in 2007 (*BurrellesLuce Top 100 List*, 2007). Yet, an unfortunate tragedy—the Virginia Tech shooting—would sadly help me find my voice as a writer.

Local: First Submission.
Rejected

A unique aspect of the Community Columnist call focused on local interests over national or global ones. As a local newspaper, the News Sentinel sought authors who could provide commentary on interests relevant to Knoxvillians and Tennesseans. National politics is a topic most folks know well, and access to national issues is on talk radio, cable news, internet outlets, and almost anywhere one turns to find news. Local politics is more challenging and not a typical dinner conversation. Thus, to have an opinion on local politics requires getting in the trenches, attending commission meetings, reading mayoral press releases, and listening to neighbors' concerns.

In 2007, I had lived in Knoxville for nearly 10 years. I married Lisa in 2004, and we started a family with the birth of our daughter Grace in 2006. I had also joined the Karns Republican Club and helped a few politicians campaign through door-to-door knocking. I had a decent handle on Knoxville's interests but was still nervous. I did not yet have my voice as a writer.

Then, unexpected tragedy struck.

On April 16, 2007, Seung-Hui Cho shot and killed 32 people on the Virginia Tech campus in Blacksburg, Virginia, before taking his own life (Research, 2024). I had received confirmation that I would write for the News Sentinel only a few weeks before, and this tragic event hit me hard. I was deeply saddened.

Scruffy Little Essays

I had already started writing the draft for my column to submit to the News Sentinel editorial staff. I was writing an article about the unfair practices of tow trucks in the Knoxville downtown area near campus known as The Strip. I had written a couple of paragraphs when I saw the news coverage of Cho's horrific murders. Not only did Cho's sadistic actions anger me, but so did the holier-than-thou finger-pointing by pundits casting blame with little to no evidence yet available. I switched gears. I started writing a whole new column, and I found my voice. The column below is the article that I submitted, and the editors asked if they could publish it immediately without waiting for my Community Columnist slot. I agreed.

I do not know the impact this article had, if any. A few family members and friends told me the article resonated with them. Beyond that, I can only say that it resonated with me.

After publishing the Virginia Tech article, I returned to the tow truck column. I later submitted the article, but the editors rejected it as potentially libelous. However, they later published a version of the tow truck article as an online-only column. I am unsure why they changed their minds; the editors never indicated why the article was published online. Both articles appear below.

Tragedy: Virginia Tech Shooting.
April 21, 2007

"To tame the savageness of man and make gentle the life of this world." Robert F. Kennedy, recalling the wisdom of the ancient Greeks, spoke these words on the night of April 4, 1968, before a crowd in one of Indianapolis' black neighborhoods (*Statement on Assassination of Martin Luther King, Jr., Indianapolis, Indiana, April 4, 1968*, 2024).

Those listening to Kennedy did not yet know the news, but that night was dark and tragic in our nation's history. That evening, on the balcony of the Lorraine Motel, an assassin's bullet extinguished the life of Dr. Martin Luther King Jr.

Kennedy stood alone before a few thousand folks, primarily men and women of color. He had planned to deliver a campaign speech but instead delivered the sad news of King's death.

That night, a swirling storm of riots engulfed cities throughout our nation, but Kennedy's words of peace calmed those who listened in Indianapolis. Years of racial oppression rapidly boiled over into many cities, and yet Indianapolis remained quiet as dawn broke.

As I watched with sadness the events that unfolded in Blacksburg, Virginia, this week, I was reminded of Kennedy and Indianapolis. When we see senseless acts of violence, our natural reaction is to lash out. Our rage drives our thoughts to seek answers. We look for someone to blame. We look for reason amid insanity.

Scruffy Little Essays

The tragedy of Blacksburg is a sad testament to man's savagery, but the subsequent outpouring of compassion is a more powerful witness to mankind's innate goodness.

Some, however, take this time of sorrow and point fingers and make accusations. They prefer to Monday-morning-quarterback Virginia Tech Police Chief Wendell Flinchum and University President Charles Steger.

Such accusing quarterbacks should take note. Cho Seung-Hui is solely responsible for the violent rampage that took the lives of 32 people. Cho is to blame, not Flinchum, not Steger.

It is easy to criticize and pass judgment from the comfortable and lofty position of hindsight. News personalities, talk-show pundits, and blogging buffoons should be ashamed. They lash out with witchhunts and cast blame, but they would be wise to heed Kennedy's counsel.

Now is not the time to riot against Flinchum or Steger. Now is the time to mourn the loss of heroes such as Liviu Librescu, who gave his life so that his students might live.

Now is not the time to crucify police chiefs or presidents. Now is the time to praise Zach Petkewicz's selflessness, which overcame fear and saved the lives of so many.

Some folks sit back and casually judge decision-makers' actions with a holier-than-thou mentality. They will tell you that they saw it all along, and they would have made better decisions.

These saw-it-all-along perceptions are common among people whose most challenging decisions on any given day are paper or plastic. Psychology researchers tell us that such hindsight judgment is faulty and is known as hindsight bias, the after-the-fact feeling that some outcome—Cho's two-hour killing spree—was predictable even though no one predicted it. This effect is even more significant when events are least plausible.

Flinchum and Steger made decisions on the morning of April 14 without malice or evil intent. They made judgments as best they could, given the knowledge at hand. Were mistakes made? Perhaps.

Could they have done better? Maybe.

Are they to blame? No! Only one person is to blame, and his name is Cho.

In time, blue-ribbon panels will form and review these events. Committees will make recommendations, and our campuses will ultimately be safer. That time will come, but now is a time to heal—a time to make gentle the life of this world.

Online: Tow Truck Mafia!
June 27, 2007

The doors fling open and rattle on their hinges. A frantic stranger, silhouetted by the noonday sun, appears, and a quiet hush falls over the once-noisy restaurant. An ominous whistle that announces a showdown in those old spaghetti westerns cuts through the silence.

With his knees quivering, the stranger calls out, "They're here! They're towing!" Fear spreads through the room.

No, it's not Black Bart or some other dastardly villain from a John Wayne movie. It's worse. It's the Tow Truck Mafia, and lunchtime on The Strip, the section of Cumberland Avenue near the University of Tennessee campus, is fertile ground for this carnivorous breed.

A panicky feeling hits your gut. Where did you park? Your mind races to double-check. The panic turns to fear, but then from fear to relief as you remember parallel parking along the street beyond the reach of the Mafia. You're safe—for now.

The Tow Truck Mafia gang trolls the private parking lots downtown for those unfamiliar. This soulless bunch masquerades as legitimate tow truck operators, but only the casual visitor falls for this deception. The more hardened regulars know the tactics of these scavengers all too well. They lurk in the shadows and secretly wait. One miscue and these vultures swoop down. They surround your car and lay their trap of extortion.

OK, I am a bit overdramatic, but if you doubt the existence of this Mafia, spend some time strolling along The Strip during the weekday lunch hour. You'll see first-time visitors, unaware of the private lots, begging for mercy as their car dangles from a tow hook. You'll see hand-scrawled signs plastered on restaurant doors that beg patrons to avoid parking over there. And yes, while eating lunch, you'll even hear strangers shouting desperate warnings, "They're towing!"

The Tow Truck Mafia can be felt almost anywhere on The Strip, but the problem is not so much the tow trucks as the private parking lots. These lots are practically empty on any given day. They attract the naive driver like the irresistible glow of a bug zapper.

Regular patrons rarely use these private lots, and they serve no useful purpose except as killing fields for the Tow Truck Mafia. I offer nothing more than anecdotal evidence, but evidence nonetheless, that these lots and the Mafia are a nuisance to Knoxville.

The Metropolitan Planning Commission recently published a study that hints at this swindling flimflam. Regarding The Strip, the MPC notes that the off-street parking lots are privately owned and tightly controlled, creating a very negative and confusing impression for visitors.

I applaud the MPC for recognizing the problem, but I fault them for not calling out the Mafia for what it is. These private lots are a sham. They are only in business for the tow truck shysters.

If a doctor tripped would-be patients at his front door and dragged them into his office for treatment, we would be outraged. Yet, the Tow Truck Mafia employs a similar modus operandi.

City officials have allowed this mafia-style environment to fester far too long. Knoxville does not need these idle parking lots—they are a waste of resources—and we don't need the Tow Truck Mafia, a machine of greed.

Knoxville can do better. Getting rid of the Mafia would create a more vibrant and inviting Strip.

CHAPTER 2

Noting Public Interests

WITH MY FIRST THREE columns, I attempted to focus less on politics and more on public interests. The first article is one that I enjoyed writing as I had good memories of my father, Bob Page, who passed away when I was 12 years old. He worked as a Vocational Rehabilitation Counselor for the State of Tennessee, and the Rehabilitation Act of 1973, a precursor to the 1990 Americans with Disabilities Act, had taken effect, giving more access and opportunities to Americans and Tennesseans with disabilities.

The most visible aspect of these laws is the handicapped parking spaces in shopping centers, grocery stores, malls, and other parking lots. Over the years, I have grown frustrated to see the apparent abuse of these privileged parking spaces, with the most appalling news being the anecdotal evidence of fraud. My outrage led me to write this first column.

The second column had a different background. I met a gentleman named Joe Ferguson, who inspired this column. In Chattanooga, I attended the Tennessee Valley Corridor Conference, which brings together regional leaders to discuss collaborations in science and technology as a catalyst for regional growth. At the conference to support my work with the University of Tennessee, I met Joe as he had stopped by our booth. We had a great conversation.

He casually commented that Atlanta airport's growth was not sustainable and that Chattanooga's airport could serve as a 'relief valve' for the traffic volumes flying to Atlanta. I was intrigued. I said, "You mean like Gatwick?"

I had recently traveled to London, England, but rather than fly into Heathrow airport, I flew to Gatwick and then traveled by train up to London. Joe understood my reference and replied, "Exactly!" He explained how he wanted to build a high-speed rail from Chattanooga to Atlanta to help unload the tremendous air travel into Atlanta. That conversation plunged me into research and led to my second column.

Finally, a news headline that I had read about lottery-based scholarships in Tennessee inspired the third article in this chapter. A proposal before the Tennessee legislature sought to lower the standards to allow more students to maintain their scholarships. After reading the news article, I bolted into action with my new-found Community Columnist soapbox. The first two articles were ones that I had planned before applying to the News Sentinel. Like the Cho article in the introduction, this third article was more reactionary and organic.

I have included the dates for each column to give a sense of the context, and I have used my original draft text rather than the edited version published in the newspaper, mainly for copyright reasons. I also had what seemed to be a clever idea to end each column with the call to action, "Are you with me?" Thankfully, I soon abandoned this catchphrase as it was clumsy and sophomoric. My growth as a writer has many bumps and bruises, and this phrase was one of them.

Parking: Handicapped or Just Lazy?
April 29, 2007

"Just place it gently under the windshield wiper," my father would say to me in a kind but disappointed voice. I knew his disappointment was not with me but with them, whoever parked their car in that space.

It was 1979, and my father worked as a state Vocational Rehabilitation Counselor. He was deeply committed to, if not passionate about, new legislation that reserved parking spaces for disabled drivers—handicapped parking.

My father carried a pre-printed pad of 'tickets' wherever we traveled, stating that these spaces were reserved for individuals with disabilities. His unofficial tickets outlined the Tennessee Disabled Drivers Law of 1975 and were a gentle reminder.

Today, I am proud of this law's impact on the quality of life for many Tennesseans. Unfortunately, the age of instant gratification and the go-go hustle of the Internet world have led to misuse. I am sure we have all witnessed it.

- An impatient teenager whips into a disabled spot off Cumberland Avenue. "No worries. I will only be a second."
- An angry middle-aged man slips into a space at West Towne Mall. "Why do they need so many handicapped slots? Give me a break!"
- A hurried soccer mom screeches into a garage near Market Square. "Shhhh, don't tell anyone. My mother is at the nursing home." Her mother's disabled placard ensures free parking.

These anecdotes are merely representative. Dr. Donna Fletcher, a Florida State University researcher in accessibility issues for people with disabilities, reports that abuse rates from 48 percent to 76 percent are typical in a 1996 study (Fletcher, 1996).

Despite such statistics, the 1975 law was not established to save a few seconds in the lives of lazy folks. It was enacted to give equal access to disabled Tennesseans.

How many more seconds are necessary for a teenager to walk a few more spaces? How large must the disabled population be to resurrect the morality of an angry man? And perhaps worst of all, why would anyone steal—pardon me, borrow—her mother's placard?

To address these problems, I suggest we enact the Lazy Drivers Law of 2007. Individuals would not need to prove a disability. They would have to admit, "I am lazy. Can you please issue me a Lazy Tag?"

Unlike the blue disabled placards, these Lazy Tags would be bright and highly visible. They would have a big 'L' emblazoned on both sides with the notation, "The driver of this vehicle is lazy. Please allow them to park anywhere."

For this privilege, lazy drivers should pay an arm and a leg. After all, that is the price some disabled Tennesseans have paid, but let's give them away for free on a trial basis.

Since the tags would be readily available, we should punish violators with a heavy hand—think Tonya Harding. We would break one leg for the first offense, two legs for the second, and permanent disability for the third. Ultimately, repeat offenders would transition towards a blue tag and would not need a Lazy Tag.

OK, maybe I'm too harsh. My father's tickets were a more rational solution but were suitable when ignorance of the law was common. Today, ignorance has given way to arrogance. Sneaking into a handicapped space has become a sport of the lazy. It's time to enact the Lazy Drivers Law of 2007.

Are you with me?

David L. Page, Ph.D.

Transit: Planes, Trains, or Automobiles?
May 27, 2007

Have you ever raced down the Papermill 500? Perhaps the Chattanooga 600 is more your style? NASCAR drivers have probably never strapped it on and barreled down these tracks, but to Knoxvillians, the Interstate 40 and I-75 raceways are all too familiar. These overcrowded highways bring new meaning to "rubbin' is racin'."

Tennessee Department of Transportation commissioner Gerald Nicely recently announced his solution to this overcrowding: toll booths (Jacobs, 2007). Nicely proposes that Tennesseans pay tolls for their NASCAR-like experience.

Tolls are a new wrinkle in the TDOT goody bag of short-term fixes. TDOT has no long-term strategy—other than more asphalt—to alleviate current and future congestion problems.

Left unchecked, the TDOT monster would consume the entire state and leave a swath of pavement in its wake. Nicely guides the reins of this monster, calling out his commands, "Make 'em bigger! Make 'em wider! And make 'em pay!" TDOT should think long-term and move beyond the asphalt beast.

Joe Ferguson of the Enterprise Center in Chattanooga has a more creative vision for Tennessee's future transportation needs: high-speed rails (Ferguson, 2007).

Ferguson, whose passion is contagious, is leading the charge for a high-speed rail to connect Chattanooga and Atlanta. The idea to link these two cities initially emerged in the late 1990s when Atlanta officials studied the need for a new airport in their northern suburbs.

The immense passenger volumes at Atlanta's Hartsfield airport have long been squeezing out local travelers. A high-speed rail would connect Lovell Field in Chattanooga to Atlanta and provide these travelers an alternative to Hartsfield.

Whoa! I can already hear the brakes squealing. Yes, building a high-speed rail would be more expensive in the short term. Early estimates put the costs at $30 million per mile (Thompson, 2004), but consider that the price tag to expand a four-lane interstate of gridlock into six lanes of more gridlock is nearly $10 million per mile. By comparison, the costs are less daunting.

The key to the money question is redistributing existing resources rather than creating new ones. We don't need to raise new money. We need to redirect priorities from wider roads and bigger airports. Hartsfield itself is expanding to the tune of $5.4 billion (Thompson, 2004).

High-speed rails also have a more acceptable revenue source in ticket fares than Nicely's unpopular tolls. No one wants to sit in bumper-to-bumper traffic and throw coins at a basket.

Ferguson, however, would have more than a few paying customers whisked to Atlanta at 250 mph. We cannot continue expanding our interstates and airports and expect to meet our future transportation needs. The current grow-as-you-go attitude is a lousy policy. Fortunately, such reactionary thinking has not always been the norm. Forward-thinking occasionally wins out.

In 1954, President Dwight Eisenhower, a true forward thinker, understood the need for a robust transportation infrastructure. He set a course to build our interstate highway system despite the costs. Nearly 40 years of construction and over $125 billion later, few would deny its value (Cox & Love, 1998).

Today, we—including TDOT—stand at a new crossroads, much like Eisenhower. Our interstates are overcrowded. We need to modernize. Planes serve long-distance needs, such as New York to San Francisco, and automobiles serve short distances, such as Knoxville to Oak Ridge. High-speed rails would fill the middle gap, such as Knoxville to Atlanta.

Maybe the "Little Engine that Could" is not as sexy as "Rubbin' is racin'," but with Ferguson's help and a broader Ike-like vision, Tennessee could step forward and lead our nation toward a new future of planes, trains, and automobiles.

Who's with me? All aboard!

Education: Rising Above Mediocrity.
June 24, 2007

The recent debate surrounding changes to lottery scholarships has reminded me of an observation by Michael Barone in his book *Hard America, Soft America* (Barone, 2005).

According to Barone, a peculiar feature of our country is that we seem to produce incompetent 18-year-olds who have difficulty making correct change at McDonald's but remarkably competent 30-year-olds who drive the most robust private-sector economy in the world.

Perhaps Barone's characterization is too harsh, but his observation is worth noting, especially in our present scholarship debate.

As the title of his book implies, Barone attributes this interesting paradox to the dichotomy of two Americas. Soft America is the world of our children from ages 6 to 18, who we protect from competition and coddle against accountability. Hard America is the dog-eat-dog world of adults where we must fend for ourselves.

Soft America plays for fun; Hard America plays for keeps.

With Barone in mind, I've read recent news articles and opinion columns with interest about the lottery scholarship debate during the recent session of the state Legislature.

The debate centers on two issues: the projected $33 million surplus that the lottery has generated this year and—the most interesting point—that three out of four students lose their scholarships due to poor grades once they are in college (Law, 2007).

To remain eligible after earning a lottery scholarship, students must maintain a 2.75 grade-point average after their first year of college and a 3.0 GPA for each subsequent year (L. I. Johnson, 2007).

In response to the large surplus and the lackluster retention rate, lawmakers in Nashville voted on a bill that would have lowered these requirements to allow more students to keep their scholarships. The bill passed in the House but failed in the Senate.

The bill failed partly due to State Senator Jamie Woodson's maneuvering, who held it until the last moment (Humphrey, 2007). Woodson argued that the bill had many good ideas but that "preparation is the key to retention."

I strongly agree with Woodson.

I can sympathize with parents and students who may lose a scholarship. Life can throw a curve ball and knock one's grades off course. Bumps in the road are not uncommon, and as a former engineering student, I can understand that some classes are more challenging than others.

Maintaining a 3.0 GPA is not an easy row to hoe for today's college students. It is difficult. Yet we must resist the ever-creeping urge to allow Soft America to erode the quality of higher education.

Today, we live in a global economy, a flat world. Tennessee's students no longer compete against their compatriots in Kentucky, North Carolina, and Georgia. Instead, they compete against their counterparts in China, India, and Germany.

We should not lower the standards of the lottery scholarship, and we should never settle for mediocrity. We should set the bar high.

Please don't get me wrong. We must encourage as many students as possible to attend college and give them every reasonable opportunity to succeed. The lottery scholarships are essential, and they are good for Tennessee. However, we must distinguish between earning a scholarship and giving one away.

The larger question we should consider is not how we can help students maintain their lottery scholarships but why they cannot retain them. Why are students who do well in high school unable to do as well in college? The uncomfortable answer may lie in transitioning from Soft America to Hard America.

CHAPTER 3

Observing Government

With a few columns under my belt, I was ready to start into my favorite subject: politics. Like most folks, I have followed national politics more closely than local. Since I first applied for the Community Columnist opportunity, I had begun to dig more into local news stories. One could not have picked a better time to investigate Knox County politics.

On January 31, 2007, the Knox County Commission held a scheduled meeting to address concerns over a recent Tennessee State Supreme Court decision that term limit provisions in Knox County's Charter should be enforced. The subsequent meeting, which included multiple recesses, corner sidebars, and other odd behaviors, became known as Black Wednesday.

The Court's ruling ousted longtime officeholders, and the Commission called a meeting to appoint replacements. Yet, the chaotic meeting did little to preserve trust in the process, as Commissions did not appoint new officeholders based on credentials or qualifications. Instead, they appointed friends, family members, and political cronies.

Black Wednesday became an infamous moment in Knox County history, and the fallout provided a wealth of material for opinion writers. With that background, I wrote the following three columns in the summer of 2007.

Trust: Restoring Faith in Commission.
July 22, 2007

Nepotism and cronyism are never isolated acts. To exist in a democracy, they require collusion and corruption of an arrogant few who exchange favors in a scratch-my-back-and-I'll-scratch-yours barter.

As such, they are not the sins of a lone renegade but are the collective transgressions of an alliance. A renegade is easy to root out, but unfortunately, an entrenched coalition is far more difficult to uproot.

Black Wednesday and this year's events witness such an alliance within the Knox County Commission. Consider the appointments of a wife, a son, and a father to fill the vacated seats. Further, 13 of the 19 current commissioners either work for or have close relatives who work for Knox County.

These commissioners and their relatives draw over $1 million in annual income from the county coffers (Editors, 2007).

These facts are embarrassing and disgraceful. Sadly, such nepotism and cronyism have eroded faith and trust in our County Commission.

As citizens of Knox County, however, we can dismantle this alliance. Next year, we can reverse these shameful appointments. With the election of eight new commissioners, we can send a clear message and establish a strong mandate for change.

To do so, I propose that each candidate pledge to the following eight reforms in 2008. This "Eight-in-'08" pledge would transform the individual district elections into a countywide referendum.

- No commissioners or their immediate family members, defined as spouses or dependents living in the same household, may accept an hourly job on the Knox County payroll unless they held it before the election. We need to stop the appearance of tit-for-tat job exchanges.
- We need an even higher standard for salaried positions. While in office, no commissioners or their immediate family members may hold salaried positions—excluding teachers—in Knox County government, regardless of whether they had that position before the election. Commissioners must choose to serve the people.
- The appointment process for county commissioners who leave office before their term expires must be overhauled. The selective

swearing-in of commissioners to manipulate votes is unacceptable and should be stopped.
- Commissioners serving on a commission committee as members or chairpersons must step down from that committee upon leaving office. They may be reappointed at the commission's pleasure, but they must first step down.
- No County Commission meeting should start before 5 p.m. The current chaos of meeting times does not allow citizens who work to attend meetings, thus veiling the commission's activities.
- The stipend of County Commissioners should be reduced from the current $19,400 per year to $14,400 per year, a reduction of $5,000 (*http://web.knoxnews.com/pdf/0525 budget_travelpay.pdf*, 2007). It is shameful that commissioners, as part-time public servants who officially meet for a few hours each month, earn more than many full-time working citizens who clock in a full 40 hours weekly. The County Commission is a public service, not a posh paycheck.
- No commissioners should be allowed to distribute $5,000 in discretionary funds (G. Johnson, 2007). Such funds should be eliminated from the budget and the process of rewards and favors.
- Commissioners should disclose all trips when they travel outside of Knox County as county representatives. Such disclosures should outline who is paying for the trip and its purpose.

These measures would go a long way to remove the cancers of nepotism and cronyism that have plagued our Commission. Together, we can remove the disgrace of Black Wednesday and restore pride in Knox County government.

Leadership: Tear Down vs. Build Up?
August 26, 2007

John Adams, one of our nation's Founding Fathers, once said of a rival that he was the sort of man to tear a house down but lacked the skills to rebuild it. A similar description seems appropriate for the current leadership of Knox County.

With each passing day, newspaper headlines report a new scandal, a new controversy, a new house falling. Infighting, finger-pointing, and name-calling are the order of the day as county officials tear down each other and thus tear down our trust in them.

The casual observer might wonder what all the fuss is about. Why has Knox County government suddenly imploded?

The short answer is simple—term limits.

Term limits have disrupted Knox County's ruling elite, and they—as one might expect—are not sitting idly by and watching as their power structure erodes. They are putting up a fight.

For many years, these elites—not in the sense of intellect or wealth but in terms of power—have carved out their niche in government and wielded their influence. They have held on to their positions at all costs.

Term limits have revealed their true character. At the moment when their leadership is needed most, they have chosen to make backroom deals instead. They have decided to retain power rather than humbly serve.

Unfortunately, Knox County's citizens have no one to blame but ourselves for this mess. We voted for them.

Thus, the question becomes, can these leaders rebuild the house? Can they put aside their power struggles and move Knox County forward?

I would argue that some can, but sadly most cannot. Most are the sort of folks who can tear a house down but cannot rebuild it. Our leadership has lost its way. Knox County is at a low point.

Yet, true leaders emerge at such moments, and it is our job as voters to diligently search for and actively support them. What should we look for? How do we recognize the leaders who are rebuilders?

Dr. Edwards Deming, a quality management guru, once said, "The aim of leadership is not merely to find and record failures in men but to remove the causes of failure." In essence, Deming says that leaders should correct processes rather than people.

Deming is our clue to identifying the leaders who can rebuild our trust in Knox County government. For example, some county leaders say that heads should roll in the P-card scandal. They argue that those employees responsible for P-card abuse should be terminated.

Perhaps, but doing so is a short-term solution. Firing people does not fully correct the problem. The P-card review process failed—not just the staff—and needs correction.

Similarly, some county leaders have called for their cohorts to step down from office for Black Wednesday. They accuse them of nepotism and cronyism, which may be true, but the process is the problem again.

Knox County does not have a clear nepotism policy, and the tit-for-tat exchange of favors will continue until such a policy comes forward.

Next year, we can elect a new group of leaders for Knox County. Our choice is clear. We can continue with the status quo and elect leaders from the power elite who have readily demonstrated how to tear a house down, or we can look for new leaders who want to rebuild it.

I urge Knox County voters to support Deming-style leaders who offer solutions to processes rather than cast accusations at people.

Polarization: The Deep Pocket Veto.
September 23, 2007

The News Sentinel is embroiled in a lawsuit against the Knox County Commission. At the heart of this legal tug-of-war are allegations that commissioners willfully violated the Tennessee Open Meetings Act, more commonly called the Sunshine Law.

The lawsuit focuses on a Jan. 31 commission meeting called Black Wednesday, during which alleged backroom deals brought relatives and cronies to replace term-limited officeholders.

While the commission's actions are disgraceful, we should be careful before embracing the News Sentinel lawsuit. The News Sentinel defines a very tenuous standard for the Sunshine Law — the two-member standard. The danger is that if the courts favor this standard, any wild-eyed lawyer with an axe to grind and deep pockets could effectively hold a veto over the County Commission.

The News Sentinel argues that if two or more commissioners discuss county business, that meeting must be public record. If not, the commissioners have violated the law and are open to lawsuits.

At first blush, this two-member standard sounds like good government, but more thoughtful considerations reveal the fallacies. Under this standard, even commissioners from the same district cannot consult one another about bridges, schools, or other matters unless they do so in a public forum. There are no phone calls, and there are no working lunches.

This standard is impractical and opens a Pandora's box for lawsuits. It's no wonder that the state Legislature exempted itself from this law.

Although the Sunshine Law's noble intentions are to eliminate good-old-boy networks, those intentions have led to this unforeseen deep-pocket veto, where high-priced lawyers can block the actions of the County Commission. We should, therefore, reconsider this law. The standard should be

Scruffy Little Essays

changed rather than just two elected body members.

In some cases, the standard might be a quorum; in others, it might be one-third of the body. The standard should be based on the number of members whose collective actions can alter the body's decisions. Such a flexible standard is more reasonable and practical yet still embodies the spirit of the Sunshine Law.

We need a standard that allows commissioners to discuss matters beyond the polarizing scrutiny of the press. Private discussions—at least within limits—are essential to a functioning elected body.

The News Sentinel may disagree, but our Founding Fathers understood this principle. Our history teachers will tell us that our great Constitution was written in secret. In 1787, a group of patriots met and drafted this important document behind closed doors. There were no reporters. There was no sunshine. George Washington served as the central enforcer.

Why the secrecy? The Founding Fathers understood that "secret discussions were imperative to foster deliberation and compromise," as former Chief Justice Warren Burger noted in his 1995 book *It Is So Ordered* (Burger, 1995).

We should heed this lesson from our Founding Fathers and Burger. We should not fear closed-door meetings but judge them by their outcomes. The Constitutional Convention's outcome was a document that has stood the test of time. By contrast, Black Wednesday's outcome is a clumsy set of appointments tarnished by nepotism.

The News Sentinel was right to expose Black Wednesday's backroom deals. Our commissioners should be held accountable in the court of public opinion, but the News Sentinel is wrong to try them in a court of law. The News Sentinel should stand as the beacon of a free press in Knox County, not as a plaintiff in a Sunshine lawsuit.

CHAPTER 4

Exploring Other Topics

AT THE YEAR-END OF 2007, I wanted to explore other topics beyond the local political headlines. The result is the following three articles. The first topic came to my attention after hearing Dr. Ed Kraft speak at a Tennessee Valley Corridor forum. The TVC, per their website, was organized in 1995 based on the ideas of former Tennessee Governor and U.S. Senator Lamar Alexander and former Tennessee Congressman Zach Wamp. While I was at the University of Tennessee, our laboratory attended these forums to demonstrate our academic research as part of the technology in the Tennessee Valley. Through these forums, I had an opportunity to meet political and thought leaders from the Tennessee Valley region. Dr. Kraft was one such leader.

After hearing Dr. Kraft's talk, I thought about my neighborhood and one of my neighbors, Marty. When Marty moved in just a few doors down from my house, I got to know him and his background in the U.S. Navy Seabees, known more formally as the Naval Construction Force. He was a noncommissioned officer, and I enjoyed listening to his Navy stories, mainly when he was stationed in Guantanamo Bay, Cuba. Marty struck me as the perfect fit for the soldier-to-teacher program that Dr. Kraft had outlined in his TVC talk and that I discuss in the article below.

The second topic, November 18, 2007, is the first time I have thought about modified school calendars in-depth. In this article, I argue that it is time to change from the current calendar with a long summer break to a calendar that spreads shorter breaks throughout the year. As I noted in a later chapter for an article on April 28, 2015, this 2007 argument was wrong. Perhaps "wrong" is too strong a word. We should not declare political arguments "right" or "wrong" as the goal is not moral correctness. Instead, political arguments aim to persuade voters towards a more optimal government. In most cases, political debates are not around right or wrong. The calendar debate over schools is such a case.

When I wrote the article below in 2007, my thinking was limited, and I had only touched the surface of the research available on balanced calendars. After publishing the article, I received an email from one reader that challenged my views and pointed me toward additional research. That research and subsequent papers changed my perspective on modified calendars. Thus, the 2007 opinion below and the follow-on one in 2015 reflect my shift in thinking and the maturation of my argument towards the creative benefits of our long-summer calendar. These benefits are mainly for middle- and upper-income students who have the resources to take advantage of summer activities beyond sitting at home.

"Change is inevitable. Growth is optional," writes John Maxwell, an American author. I would not say I like changing my mind. I want to dig in and hold my position. In this case, the email challenge I received was evidence I could not ignore. Maxwell's quote and Keynes' quote earlier in this book comfort my stubborn mind.

Finally, Christmas inspired me to write something more light-hearted for the third piece. I had given a few talks at the University of Tennessee about robotics and how we are not quite able to make the robots of our fictional movies, such as Star Wars C3P0. In those talks, I broke down the numbers of where we, as scientists and engineers, stood in being able to build C3P0 and other human-like robots. Those talks led me to the article that I wrote.

In 2024, we are now 17 years past the time I wrote this article, and we are a little closer to C3P0 but still far, far away. In this column, I point out that we do not have a good understanding of the software of the human mind. Well, now we do. With the growth of knowledge in neural networks and deep learning frameworks, we have a much better understanding of the software of the human mind. What's the next missing puzzle? I would point to embodiment. To better understand embodiment, I would guide the interested reader to Scott Grafton's book *Physical Intelligence* (Grafton, 2020). With that background, please enjoy the next three columns.

Neighborhoods: Soldiers to Teachers.
October 21, 2007

Does your neighborhood have its own NCO? Mine does, and his name is Marty. We are more than glad to have him.

If you don't know, NCO is military speak for a noncommissioned officer. These men and women are the backbone of our modern armed forces. They are highly skilled, highly trained individuals who are the military's plant-floor managers—to use an industry term. NCOs are where the rubber meets the road.

Before retiring, Marty was a member of the Seabees, the engineering and construction battalion of the U.S. Navy. As a Seabee, Marty led young soldiers to build bridges and bulldoze mountains. With more than 20 years of military experience, he and his family lived on the East Coast, the West Coast, and all ports in between.

Now a civilian, Marty has transformed our ragtag neighborhood of do-it-yourselfers into an army of handymen that could give the DIY channel a run for its money. Marty has translated both his construction and leadership skills into making our neighborhood a better place.

He has done such a great job that our wives have stopped nagging us about our honey-do lists. On any given weekend, you will find Marty side by side with one of my neighbors hammering nails on a deck, laying sod for a lawn, or sawing two-by-fours for a fence.

So why do I bring this up?

If Dr. Ed Kraft, chief technologist at the U.S. Air Force Arnold Engineering Development Center in Tullahoma, Tenn., has his way, Tennessee neighborhoods will soon have their own NCO, just like our Marty.

Kraft is co-director of the NCO Enhanced Workforce in Science, Technology, Engineering, and Mathematics, a part of the Tennessee Valley Corridor Educational Initiative (Kraft, 2007). The NEW-STEM initiative leverages the Troops to Teachers Program at the federal level and looks like a political win-win program. Kraft, through NEW-STEM, proposes a creative way to link two crucial needs.

The first need involves NCOs. Over the next five years, the U.S. military will see a dramatic change in force levels due to doctrine shifts and budgetary constraints. This force shaping—the military term for restructuring—will lead to thousands of military personnel, particularly NCOs, separating from service. These folks will be looking for jobs outside the military and new places to live.

The second need, particularly in Tennessee, is the gap in math and science teachers in the K-12 pipeline. In 2005, the National Academy of Sciences released a critical report titled "Rising above the Gathering Storm" (Science et al., 2007). This report clearly states that the U.S. is losing its competitive edge, and a key finding is the lack of qualified math and science teachers.

Kraft's vision is to bring these two needs together through NEW-STEM. NCOs separating from the military are perfect candidates to be Tennessee's math and science teachers of tomorrow.

NCOs have a proud history of turning immature, selfish 18-year-olds into highly motivated, selfless soldiers. With high-tech military backgrounds, NCOs are prepared to teach our YouTube-MySpace-blogosphere teenagers how to compete in the nano-biogenetic-dot-com global economy.

We are facing a crisis in math and science education. We are on a self-destructive path if we do not change course soon. Kraft and NEW-STEM offer a window of hope and opportunity.

The military crucible has forged NCOs into leaders of young men and women, and nomadic military life has necessitated good-neighbor humor in their families. Marty has transformed my neighborhood; NCOs like him can transform Tennessee's schools.

Progress: Asking "Why?"
November 18, 2007

One hundred and eighty days. That is the number of school days in the traditional Knox County school calendar. Most folks don't realize that it is also precisely the same number of school days in the so-called year-round calendar, which is a misleading term.

The traditional calendar has a long summer break, while the year-round calendar spreads breaks throughout the year. More but shorter breaks with the year-round calendar attempt to overcome summer regression and thus maximize learning retention. The traditional calendar, conversely, has a less rational justification.

Most arguments supporting traditional calendars remind me of a conversation between a young girl and her mother about baking a ham.

"Cut the ends off the ham and place it in the pan," instructs the mother.

"Why?" questions the daughter. "Why cut the ends off?"

"We've always done it that way," replies the mother. "That's how my mother taught me."

Unsatisfied, the little girl trots over to her grandmother and asks the same question, but to her disappointment, the grandmother offers a similar answer.

The little girl, still unsatisfied, huffs over to her great-grandmother and again asks why. The great-grandmother replies, "My sweet child, what a silly question; my baking pans were always too small. I had to cut the ends off for the ham to fit."

With that in mind, our schools operate on an agrarian calendar that dates back over 200 years. In those days, children worked on the family farm during the summers, and the school year, ironically, was their vacation. Today, both parents typically work outside the home—not a farm—with no summer breaks, yet our schools still follow the harvest cycle.

Why?

The most common retort is an appeal to nostalgia—the good old days. Like the mother baking the ham, we've always done it that way. After all, what evil person wants to steal summers away from our children? One statewide organization against year-round calendars even declares that we must "Save Tennessee Summers!" as if the Grinch is on his way.

These emotional pleas create a false dilemma and polarize the debate between those no-good folks who want to steal summer and those supposed do-gooders who wish to save it. We must avoid this fallacy. Instead, we should debate what calendar best equips our children.

Many teachers spend several weeks each fall reviewing last year's material to overcome summer regression, but evidence suggests that year-round calendars reduce this problem. Harris Cooper, a professor at Duke University who has studied the effects of modified calendars, says that students in year-round schools rate higher in learning retention (Cooper, 2004).

Additionally, if we again consider the typical family, year-round calendars fit their lifestyle better. Most children do not have a parent at home over the summer; thus, they sit idly playing "Guitar Hero" and munching on cheesy puffs.

Some folks alternatively argue that year-round calendars create daycare hardships and destroy summer camps. No worries. Our robust market economy and Adam Smith's invisible hand will quickly adjust. Just imagine fall, winter, and spring camps.

Finally, considering the global context, quibbling over ways to carve 180 days seems trivial. Students in India, for example, attend school for 225 days—equivalent to three additional years over a K-12 career—and in China for 250 days—nearly five extra years equivalent to a college degree.

So, as Knox County debates calendar options, we need to cast aside emotional arguments about saving Tennessee summers and engage in a more thoughtful debate. More importantly, we must be like the little girl who engages her mother about the ham and asks why.

Future: Robots?
December 23, 2007

Many gadget geeks like me will be excited to unwrap their latest robot toys on Christmas morning. This year, options range from Roomba to Robosapien.

Soon after the New Year, however, this initial excitement will wear off as one realizes that these robots fall far short of our Hollywood expectations. Our toys never fulfill our hopes of having our own R2 unit, like Luke Skywalker.

Why is that? Why are our engineers unable to replicate even the most rudimentary intelligence? The answer to that question has more to do with the miracle of life than with the intellect of engineers.

We can build the components necessary to achieve a human-like robot in many ways. For example, consider the muscles of our bodies. Since the Industrial Revolution, we have built machines and motors with far greater speed and lifting capacity than humans. Muscles are not the problem.

Next, consider the human eye. Over the last three decades, digital imaging has made huge leaps and bounds toward higher resolution and smaller devices. In our homes, we have seen digital cameras replace film cameras, and the term "megapixel," which measures the resolution and thus the quality of a digital camera, has replaced "Kodak" in our vocabularies.

Most folks now own cameras with several megapixels. A natural question is what the megapixel equivalent for our eyes is. Although the answer is not straightforward, most researchers would argue that our eyes are virtually a 300-megapixel camera. This number is larger than most Wal-Mart cameras, and yet it is not beyond our technology. Our eyes are not the limiting factor in our quest.

Finally, consider our brain. The brain is the computer of our bodies. The fundamental computational element of the brain is a neuron, and communication between neurons defines the brain's fundamental speed. To process information, neurons fire and send signals across a synaptic gap to communicate with other neurons in the brain. This synaptic process requires about one millisecond.

Scruffy Little Essays

Can our present-day computers go faster than that? The exciting answer is that, yes, they can. The fundamental computational element of a modern computer is a transistor, and the clock speed of a laptop defines the communication delay from one transistor to another. Most folks own a computer with a one or two-gigahertz clock speed. Thus, the transistor-to-transistor speed for an average desktop computer is about one million times faster than the neuron-to-neuron speed of the brain.

How can that be? How can a computer be faster than our brain? That seems to go against our experience. The answer to this seeming paradox is that the computer is a sequential machine while our brain is highly parallel. A laptop does one computation very fast, but our brain can do a trillion such computations simultaneously. Thus, the collective parallelism of the brain is by far quicker than a modern computer, roughly one billion times faster, if not more.

In essence, we have the necessary hardware to duplicate humans' capabilities. Our technology includes muscles, eyes, and neurons. We don't yet have the software to replicate the massive parallelism of the mind. We understand the hardware of the brain, but we are far from understanding the software of the mind.

Such geek-speak is probably boring to most readers, but as an engineer, I am constantly amazed and challenged by the miracle of life. We should pause at the wonder of creation as we wait for our Roombas and Robosapiens' batteries to recharge this holiday season.

CHAPTER 5

Digging into Politics

THE KICKOFF TO A new year in 2008 led me back to politics for my final three columns. The first one in this series is about the so-called Sunshine Laws. These laws are regulations that seek to legislate transparency and impose disclosure requirements on government activities, i.e., to bring "sunshine" onto government affairs. These laws appear to be a good idea on first consideration. However, a dangerous side effect exists that goes unnoticed. This side effect is the squelching of healthy debate. The sunshine encourages grandstanding where debate takes second fiddle to egos and polarization.

In this first column, I argued against Sunshine Laws and continue to hold this position today. The current polarization, which began to emerge in

2007 and we now see at the national level, has many causes, but a key reason is overexposure to the Internet and social media. These avenues have brought more "sunshine" into our public forum, creating a blinding effect and squashing good debate at the hands of outlandish wars of words.

The second column concerns a local basketball player on the University of Tennessee team, Dane Bradshaw. I had watched Bradshaw play in games throughout his college career, and his grit and hustle inspired me. I wanted to write about him, and this column idea came to me as I read the local news about challenges with leadership in Knox County, particularly in light of the Black Wednesday debacle.

I must confess that I had run out of steam for my final article. Writing a column once a month was tough for me. I admire professional columnists who have more frequent deadlines. The challenge is difficult to have a new column idea, a new insight, a twist on accepted knowledge, and then to condense that new perspective into a coherent written column.

For this final column, I returned once again to education. My daughter Grace attended a private school called Tate's School of Discovery. I noticed small but essential differences in her education compared to other children in public schools. This difference inspired me to write this column, but I could not capture the ideas I wanted to communicate.

As I reread this article today, I was unhappy with its message, and I could detect my laziness as the end of my 12-month column commitment approached. Sadly, this column is the one the New Sentinel framed and gave to me as a commemorative gift.

Deliberations: Public vs. Private?
January 20, 2008

The adage to be careful what you wish for is good advice when considering the Tennessee Open Meetings Act, also known as the Sunshine Law. The common perception is that this law is good, especially in light of the ousting of the Black Wednesday appointees in Knox County, but we should be careful about embracing it.

In a previous column, I argued that the Sunshine Law enables a deep-pocket veto, whereby anyone with enough money to support a lawsuit could effectively veto the County Commission. The recent Sunshine lawsuit over the Midway Business Park is a foreboding example (Flory, 2007).

The possibility of a veto is one reason the Sunshine Law is flawed legislation. A more important reason is that the law has an unintended consequence—the debasing of deliberations.

While public deliberations have apparent benefits, such as exposing good old-boy networks, they do not necessarily improve the quality of deliberations. Posturing and grandstanding are common traits of public deliberations, which lead to polarization rather than collaboration. County Commissioners will likely refrain from expressing their true thoughts and withhold honest discussion under the intensity of "sunshine."

Dr. David Stasavage, a professor of politics at New York University, has studied the drawbacks and benefits of public deliberations among elected officials. He concludes, "Contrary to received wisdom, private deliberation will, in many cases, actually be more effective than public deliberation" (Stasavage, 2004).

The central problem is that the Sunshine Law becomes unintentionally a Spotlight Law. Constant media glare from newspapers, talk radio, and newscasts polarize issues and galvanize egos into light and dark, good and evil, us against them. Rather than fostering debate, the spotlight stifles it.

In recent months, finger-pointing and name-calling on the Commission have been evidence of this spotlight effect. We have heard calls such as "he's the mayor's man!" or "they are the sheriff's boys."

I am not suggesting the Sunshine Law is unnecessary—commissioners must ultimately subject themselves to public questioning—but we need to modify the law. In particular, we need to allow two commissioners to meet beyond the spotlight. This modification is reasonable and, as Stasavage suggests, leads to better government.

We have a troubling trend in this country—from Watergate to Whitewater—of making laws that are political traps for snaring elected officials when we disagree with them. This trend allows individuals to accomplish in the jury box what they cannot accomplish at the ballot box. A stringent Sunshine Law is such a trap.

I respectfully disagree with Jack McElroy, the News Sentinel editor, who argues that the Sunshine Law has avoided such traps because of selective enforcement (McElroy, 2007)He argues that benevolence and inconvenience have stymied abuse of the law, but that slope is slippery.

I do not defend the actions of the Knox County Commission, which led to McElroy's Sunshine Lawsuit. Those actions were wrong and represented private collusion beyond just two commissioners. The jury—which ironically deliberated in private—delivered the correct verdict.

The reality, however, is that the verdict has not changed much in Knox County. Only an election—not a stringent Sunshine Law—will solve the county's woes.

The Sunshine Law now provides an easy legal weapon for those who disagree with the County Commission, but we should decide public policy through elections, not prosecutions.

This well-intentioned law encourages the misleading illusion that total transparency equals better government. We should be careful about what we wish for.

Leadership: Dane Bradshaw.
February 17, 2008

Knox County Commission needs a Dane Bradshaw—an unselfish leader who can restore faith in our government.

You know you have arrived when your name, usually a proper noun, enters our daily lexicon as a common noun. Such is the case with Bradshaw. At local basketball games, fans often suggest, "What this team needs is a Dane Bradshaw."

Bradshaw was a standout basketball player with the University of Tennessee last year. His versatility enabled him to play an uncommon combination of point guard and power forward.

Surprisingly, Bradshaw was a standout, not because he was a stellar athlete. He was not particularly tall, though he played taller than his 6'4" frame, and he was not particularly fast, though his clever play compensated for his lack of lightning speed.

Bradshaw's former teammate, Duke Crews, once said, "He's not the quickest guy. He's not the strongest guy. He's not the biggest guy, but 10 times out of 10, he seems like the smartest guy on the court" (Davis, 2007).

Bradshaw's uniqueness is not in his talent but his character and work ethic. In an age of prima donnas, his humility and hustle are rare commodities, and these traits have endeared him to Big Orange fans.

With ordinary talent, he has achieved extraordinary things. To say that someone is a Dane Bradshaw has become a compliment above reproach. His name is synonymous with someone who is unselfish, humble, and hardworking—someone who puts his team above himself.

On Wednesday, the Knox County Commission will meet to fill eight vacant commission seats. This meeting is essentially a do-over of a previous meeting—the infamous Black Wednesday on Jan. 31, 2007.

Black Wednesday is also a new name that has sadly entered the lexicon of Knox County. Unlike Dane Bradshaw, however, Black Wednesday has become synonymous with selfishness, arrogance, and the easy road.

Over the past year, Black Wednesday has come to symbolize the ineptitude of our current commissioners, who are known more for their scandals than their accomplishments.

Without a doubt, the drama that has unfolded each month during commission meetings has been entertaining, but to what end? We have seen a tug-of-war unfold each month between commissioners and the mayor. Both sides have waged a scorched-earth policy—a winner-take-all death match. Caught in the middle is our county.

With the upcoming appointments on Feb. 20, a new group of leaders will have the opportunity to step forward for Knox County. These new leaders have a choice. They can continue the status quo and keep the wheels of county government spiraling out of control. Or they can choose to be a Dane Bradshaw and humbly set a new course for Knox County.

Our County Commission, like the world of college athletics, has enough prima donnas. Many of our current commissioners prefer to be politicians rather than public servants. Our commission has few, if any, Dane Bradshaws. It doesn't have to be this way. Leaders with the Bradshaw traits of humility and hard work could transform our commission. Commission meetings wouldn't be as entertaining, but Knox County would be better off.

What if our commissioners sought consensus rather than division? What if our commissioners pursued inclusion rather than exclusion? What if our commissioners fought for Knox County rather than against each other?

Bruce Pearl, the UT head basketball coach, said of Bradshaw, "I will never miss a player more than I'll miss Dane" (Davis, 2007). Can the same be said for our current commissioners? As time passes, will they be missed?

Education: Obsolete Schools?
March 23, 2008

"America's high schools are obsolete," according to Bill Gates, the techno-savvy guru who co-founded Microsoft (Gates, 2005). Gates concludes that our schools are not broken, flawed, or underfunded, as common wisdom goes (Greene & Symonds, 2006). Instead, our schools cannot teach children what they need to know even when the schools are working exactly as designed.

At a local level, Mitch Steenrod, chief financial officer of Pilot Travel Centers, has come to a similar conclusion. In a recent News Sentinel column (Steenrod, 2008), Steenrod writes that the "retooling and re-engineering of the educational curriculum must begin, and it must begin quickly." Gates and Steenrod are noteworthy in light of the proposed academy models for the new Hardin Valley Academy and the revamped Fulton and Austin-East high schools (Alapo, 2008).

Business leaders such as Gates and Steenrod know all too well that our schools are not adequately preparing our young folks—our future workforce—for a global information-based economy. When Gates and Steenrod look for new talent to fill jobs, they come up empty-handed.

The call for change not only comes from business leaders but educators as well. John Gatto, an award-winning teacher in New York City's public schools, wrote a controversial book in 1992 called *Dumbing Us Down* (Gatto, 2002).

Gatto's conclusions are up for debate, but he convincingly argues that our schools are designed for mass education, where individuals are taught to conform to the needs of mass manufacturing. To Gatto, our schools are perfect for the industrial age.

Unfortunately, we no longer live in such an age. We now live and work in an information age. The world has changed, but our schools have not.

First, consider that our schools currently treat education as a manufacturing process. As students move along an assembly line of classes, schools attempt to add a component here (say, math) and add a component there (say, English). Like an industrial factory, a bell rings, and students move to the next classroom.

The hope is that students will somehow reassemble these classes, taught out of context, into a coherent whole. Of course, this assembly line approach is absurd. Students are not like widgets that we can assemble on demand.

Additionally, consider the curriculum of our schools. Two topics that are common in Tennesseans' daily lives are rarely found, if at all, in our public schools: risk management and financial planning.

We must look no further than today's headlines to see our schools' failure in these areas. How many Tennesseans lack health care coverage? How many Tennesseans face foreclosure on their homes? Why do so many Tennesseans carry a balance on high-interest credit cards? Why does Tennessee have one of the highest rates of personal bankruptcy?

What can we do in Knox County? Should we radically restructure our entire school system? The short answer is no, but we can and should start smaller.

We can support the academy models proposed for Hardin Valley, Fulton, and Austin-East. These academies are modest but essential in exploring new ways to educate our children. We should listen to Gates, Steenrod, and Gatto.

CHAPTER 6

Publishing the Unpublished

WITH THE SUCCESS OF my 2007-2008 Community Columnist articles behind me, I have been empowered to continue my writing as embodied in the articles in this chapter. Unfortunately, I did not submit these articles for formal publication. The opinion pieces below are ones that I wrote after 2008 to submit to the News Sentinel for publication, but I did not do so for a variety of reasons.

The one exception is the last article from April 8, 2017. This article is one that I wrote after attending Space Camp in Huntsville, Alabama, with my daughter and her classmates at Tate's School of Discovery for a weekend camp. While I did not submit this article to the News Sentinel, I gave it to the Tate's staff, who published a version on their website.

David L. Page, Ph.D.

Politics: Staying Humble.
November 22, 2008

"Stay hungry, but stay humble." Ten years ago, I heard these words as Al Wilson, a standout linebacker for the University of Tennessee, encouraged his teammates to focus on their national championship goal.

Wilson's words are not only wise counsel to young men on the gridiron, where success readily breeds dangerous arrogance, but they are equally crucial to statesmen on the political stage, where more power is often a precursor to corruption.

Tennessee Republicans, as they celebrate their recent victory for historic control of the state legislature, should heed Wilson's advice. Not since 1869 and the days of Reconstruction has the GOP controlled both the Tennessee House and Senate (Humphrey, 2008). They now have an opportunity to lead humbly or succumb to self-importance if they do not listen to Wilson.

Tennessee Republicans need to look no further than the coinciding national elections to understand the trap of self-importance. Led by Barack Obama, the national Democratic Party has ushered in a sea change to the American political landscape.

This power shift is somewhat surprising but not unexpected. Not too long ago—1994, to be more precise—the Republicans, led by Newt Gingrich, also ushered in a sea change. The 1994 elections paralleled the 2008 elections, except the national parties switched leading roles. The Republicans then, as the Democrats now, offered a new path and new leadership.

What happened? How did the Gingrich revolution give way to the Obama reversal? And what can Tennessee Republicans learn from history?

The short answer is arrogance.

The Republicans ran in 1994 on a well-defined platform of smaller government, lower taxes, and reduced spending. They delivered on these promises for a time, but their successes proved too seductive. Their leadership has become more known for Abramoff scandals, K Street lobbyists, and pork barrel earmarks.

By 2008, the Republican conservatism of 1994 had succumbed to Republican corruption. In essence, Democrats did not win the 2008 national elections as much as Republicans had lost them, which is instructive to the Tennessee GOP.

The conservative values from 1994 are still alive today. The right path is still smaller government, lower taxes, and reduced spending. Bill Clinton was right when he said, "The era of big government is over" (Krauthammer, 1999).

The Republicans, at least at the national level, have the wrong leadership. They have lost their way.

Conversely, Democrats have fresh new faces in leadership, and President-elect Obama is perhaps the best example of these new leaders. Obama has sparked a new fire in the Democratic Party that has not been seen since the days of John Kennedy, but the Obama campaign is also the best evidence that conservatism is still the right path.

In the March 2008 issue of The American Conservative, Andrew Bacevich argues the conservative case for Obama (Bacevich, 2008). Bacevich writes, "For conservatives, Obama represents a sliver of hope. McCain represents none at all. The choice turns out to be an easy one."

Whether one voted for Obama or McCain, this quote is enlightening that a heavily conservative magazine would even attempt a positive spin towards Obama. If one looks under the covers, Bacevich's article is more an indictment of the Republican leadership than an endorsement of Obama.

As columnist Ryan Lizza points out in the November issue of The New Yorker, the Obama campaign instinctively understood this downward spiral of Republican leaders (Rizza, 2008). At the outset of their campaign, Obama strategists obsessively focused on defining Obama as "not Bush."

While some pundits might argue that Obama's enigmatic message of "change" propelled him to the White House, the Obama campaign would tell you that Barack was not Bush.

Thus, Obama's historic election is a valuable lesson for the new Republican Legislature in Tennessee. The 1994 Republican revolution held great promise, but that promise gave way to corruption. Tennessee Republicans will hopefully not repeat this sad mistake of their national brethren.

Under the former leadership of Democrats, our state now faces a possible $800 million spending shortfall (Schelzig, 2008). Equally troubling, Tennessee's unemployment rate may reach nearly

9 percent (Humphrey, 2008a). In such grim times, we need leaders who understand that we voted for them to serve the people and not to serve themselves. Like Al Wilson, we ask the party of Lincoln—my party—to stay hungry but stay humble.

Local: Judging Others.
April 9, 2010

Bill Lockett is a good man in the balance of life. Commissioner Mark Harmon seems to wish he had become a good man sooner. To quote Harmon, "I wished he would've resigned when this all came out."

Harmon is referring to the transgressions of Lockett embezzling money from his former employer. Those actions and their subsequent public discovery led to Lockett's guilty plea yesterday.

Few men in this world intend to wrong their fellow man. Few men are genuinely evil. The names of actual evil that do come to mind are Hitler, Stalin, and Manson—evil men.

Few men slip into this abyss and accompany these damned souls.

Most men make mistakes during the struggle that we call life. They are not evil. Unfortunately, the burdens of life may seduce them to less-than-noble actions. The names that come to mind are Nixon, Clinton, and Woods.

This latter group of men is where most of us fall when we fall. We rarely intend genuine harm, and the balance of our moral scale readily tips to the good.

Most men are good.

We—the society surrounding these men—should not judge them merely by the depths of their wrongs. We should instead judge them—and therefore ourselves—by how they right their wrongs.

Bill Lockett has done wrong. However, he has taken the first steps towards righting his wrongs and making amends with society. These new steps are how we should judge Lockett.

He has accepted his punishment: repayment of what he stole, resignation from his elected position, and designation as a convicted felon for life.

These punishments are proper and reasonable. Now, we should begin accepting Lockett back into our society. He must ultimately fulfill his punishment, but we should not pile on.

In particular, Commissioner Harmon's snide political comments are somewhat sanctimonious. Harmon's comments are a common retort of those pious souls who sit in glass houses. The names that come to mind are Pat Robertson and Ken Starr.

Yes, Lockett did wrong. Yes, he should be punished. Yet, an easy refrain is to say he should have stepped forward sooner, or a close cousin is to say he only did it because he got caught.

Though these statements hold much truth, I am reminded of the prodigal son coming home. This well-known parable from Jesus' teachings tells about a man and his two sons. The youngest son leaves home with his share of his inheritance and wastes his father's wealth with riotous living.

Shamed, the youngest son returns home expecting his father's scowl. Instead, upon his return, the father receives him with open arms and with such joy that he throws a party.

The elder son did not react as kindly and was filled with resentment. I can almost hear the elder now, "I wished he would have done it sooner."

Education: I Was Wrong.
April 28, 2015

When I first looked at the Year-Round Calendar, a Balanced Calendar, it seemed like a great idea. In fact, in 2007, I wrote a column for the Knoxville News Sentinel arguing that Knox County Schools should adopt one.

I was wrong.

The move to a Year-Round Calendar is a mistake, and I hope Knox County is wise enough not to make it.

One of the central arguments for the Year-Round Calendar is summer regression. After a long summer break, teachers must spend several weeks reviewing last year's material. This review is inefficient; a shorter summer break would eliminate this problem (Bents, 2002).

Sounds extraordinarily logical and reasonable, right?

That's exactly what I thought. My brain, however, made a classic "thinking" error, which Daniel Kahneman discusses in his 2011 book "Thinking Fast and Slow" (Daniel, 2017).

Kahneman explains that our brains have two modes of thinking: the first is fast, instinctive, and emotional, and the second is slower, more deliberate, and more logical. Our fast thinking tends to dominate our lives, dragging the slow thinking along for the ride.

In 2007, my fast mode immediately formed an opinion, and then my slow mode had to find logical reasons for support. Our slow thinking and the associated cerebral activity give us the illusion that our views are rational and well-conceived. Yet, it is only an illusion, as emotion often nudges our initial opinion (Lehrer, 2010).

Yes, it would be nice if we would spend more time looking at both sides of an argument, withholding judgment, carefully weighing the pros and cons, and only then forming an unbiased opinion. Unfortunately, we are not wired that way.

Kahneman has helped me swallow my pride and take a second look at modified calendars. I hope the Knox County School Board will also take the time to study the issue with a little slow thinking.

The first error in fast thinking that the Board will discover is that research on modified calendars is, at best, mixed and, at worst, fails to show any advantage. More importantly, to the extent that summer regression is an issue (primarily among low-income students), modified calendars are not the solution (Kohn, 2024).

Paul Von Hippel, a sociologist at Ohio State University, asserts, "Year-round schools don't solve the problem of the summer learning setback—they simply spread it out across the year" (Von Hippel, 2007).

Thus, the original argument for Year-Round Calendars is wrong. This is to say that two students—one on a modified calendar and one on a traditional calendar, all things being equal—will learn the same amount.

The second common error is that our traditional calendar harks back to the days when most East Tennesseans were farmers. This error is not so much wrong as a fallacy in logic.

The thinking goes like this: The traditional calendar is based on a harvest cycle. Since we are no longer farmers, a harvest-based calendar is bad for our schools.

To understand this fallacy, let me illustrate with an analogy. The wheel is based on technology from ancient farmers. Since we are no longer farmers, it is a bad idea for modern man to use it.

We can all agree that wheels are great, and the mere fact that they were developed in ancient times says little about their utility.

Finally, Board members should be careful not to throw the baby out with the bathwater. Summer breaks are a valuable educational opportunity for children. Granted, they are not traditional book-learning education, but classroom tests do not measure the creative skills that children gain during summer breaks.

Michael Barone, in his 2004 book "Hard America, Soft America," tells us that America produces the worst (on standardized tests) 18-year-olds in the world but somehow magically produces the best (most creative) 30-year-olds (Barone, 2005).

While our schools lag the world in high scores on standardized tests, we lead the world in creative, out-of-the-box thinkers. Acknowledging Barone, I cannot help but wonder what magical role summer breaks have played in our children's creative development.

Maybe we need a little more slow thinking over the summer rather than some fast thinking about the harvest cycle.

Science: Confessions.
March 2, 2017

It's that time of year when the Science Fair rolls around. For almost 15 years, I have served as a Science Fair judge, and one of my main challenges has been to discern the tea leaves and how much a parent has dipped their hand into their child's science project.

It's an unwritten—but not unspoken—rule that Science Fair judges must sniff out the overbearing parent. The integrity of science hangs in the balance. We must find that project where Mom and Dad did too much.

The shoe has been on the other foot for the past two years. My ten-year-old daughter is now a Science Fair competitor, and I have struggled to walk that fine line—helping enough to kindle passion but not too much to breed apathy.

As a scientist, I love Science Fair. I love how science takes center stage. I love the enlightenment that the scientific method brings. I love the inquiry of asking questions and finding answers. The creativity. The ingenuity. The science.

Yes, I am a nerd. I am a geek. And I love how the Science Fair brings a little glory—if only a little glory—to the "smart kids" and to the kids that never thought they were "smart."

As a judge, I love to see the twinkle of science in a child's eye when you ask a tricky question, and they are ready. They have the answer, and they know it. They are confident, and the world is suddenly a better place—if not for that moment, then at least for their future. Science wins, and we win.

As a parent, I want to see that same twinkle in my daughter's eye, to see her love science the way I do, and to see that same passion. And the burden that these desires bring is palpable. I understand fully how a parent can unknowingly walk down the path that pushes a child away from science.

All this angst over a Science Fair project? Too much drama? Perhaps.

Yet, it has led me to a realization that I hope can guide me. My role in guiding her through science seems not unlike a coach's role in guiding a quarterback through football, a pitcher through baseball, or a point guard through basketball.

With sports, no one questions if the parent has done too much when the quarterback throws a tight spiral on a 10-yard-out pattern. No one questions if the dad has done too much when the pitcher strikes out the last batter in the bottom of the ninth. No one questions if the mom has done too much when the point guard drains a three from the parking lot.

It's after the game that the has-gone-too-far parent reveals themselves. The cliche of the over-involved parent is all too familiar in sports, but unlike the Science Fair, we never seem to judge the child's performance for the parent's "being too helpful." We don't impose the sin of the parent on the child.

Does that 10-yard-out deserve a penalty flag because the quarterback's parent owns a chain of workout gyms? Should that last strikeout not count if the dad played minor league ball? Should the three-pointer only be worth two points since the mom was a Lady Vol standout?

With this analogy, such penalties on the child seem silly, yet we do just that at Science Fair. We penalize the child if the parent does too much or, more often than not, if the parent is a scientist or owns a cylcospectomatograph.

With that realization—and I must confess that I may be wrong in my approach, but I hope not—I have taken a new approach to judging projects. I no longer question if a parent did too much. Instead, I ask if the child did enough. Did the child's engagement and involvement reflect an appropriate effort?

I now look for projects where a parent and child have worked together. What an excellent path of joint discovery—the path of mentor and mentee.

Yes, the dad is a world-class scientist and has access to a spectrometer. Yes, the mom is an executive at a pharmaceutical lab and has access to a fixed-angle centrifuge. What an excellent opportunity for their child.

I now resist the urge to say that's unfair to the other children. Instead, I try to discern whether the parent was fair to their child. I avoid judging the project as a whole; I try to judge simply the child's engagement.

We should encourage parents to engage their children in science and not stigmatize such engagements.

As a Science Fair judge, my role is not to discern whether a father and son tossed the basketball together. My role is to judge that the child threw the basketball. Whether his dad was involved or he used his dad's big league mitt is of little importance.

While the nuance of this realization may be of little value to others, the subtlety has become enormous to me as I learn how to coach my daughter in science.

Learning: A Questioning Mind.
April 8, 2017

"Excuse me, sir. Are you an astronaut?" asked the young server at Pizza Hut during our lunch stop for our return bus trip from Huntsville to Knoxville. We were at the South Pittsburg exit of I-24, and Grace and I had just sat down at a table in our Space Camp outfits.

My blue flight suit with NASA patches sprinkled from head to toe, my handsome good looks, and my athletic physique had misled the server. Okay, perhaps the lighting was terrible, and I am exaggerating the good looks and physique a tiny bit, but the flight suit does have a magical effect on folks, as it's a catalyst for their imaginations.

While I was flattered to be associated with the elite club of the Right Stuff, I had to confess as I blushed with embarrassment that I wasn't an astronaut but was merely a Dad returning—not from space—but from Space Camp.

Grace and I explained that our school, Tate's School of Discovery, had just spent the past three days in the Pathfinder Program at Space Camp. With a rush of enthusiasm, Grace told the tales of how we saw giant rockets, traveled in simulators, learned space history, and explored our dreams.

What a wonderful experience we had with our two fourth-grade teachers (Ms. Clark and Ms. McRae), 21 other student cadets, and 17 other parent chaperones. I am unsure who had more fun—the teachers, the students, or the parents. The smiles on our Facebook feeds are the best evidence.

While the experience was amazing, I noticed the impact Tate's has had on our children—not just in fourth grade but the accumulation of the values that Tate's has brought to our children over the years. These observations are what I want to share as they are genuinely heartwarming for me as a parent.

Flexible and Supportive

As one can imagine, a school trip spanning many days and miles will have hiccups along the way, and the diversity of the children, parents, and our individual needs could have further complicated—and potentially exacerbated—these moments.

Successful business and life managers tell us that the key is not a rigid structure to avoid these hiccups—an impossibility—but rather a flexible nature to adapt to them. I have often heard Tate's teachers talk to the children through each grade about such flexibility, particularly the need to support others as hiccups arise.

I saw this mantra in action at Space Camp; the children were fantastic. Our simulated Space Shuttle missions are perhaps the best evidence of this awesomeness.

An essential element of these missions is "Caution and Warning" anomalies. These events are random mishaps—hiccups, really—that can occur anywhere during the mission. The children must go off-script and handle each event before returning to their mission timeline.

Almost 25 years ago, I worked as a Space Camp counselor. I spent many weeks training children in these Space Camp missions, and I noticed that the children's lack of flexibility could quickly devolve into finger-pointing arguments.

Such arguments did not occur with our children. That is not to say that Tate's children were not frustrated or disappointed if they could not handle the anomalies successfully—some teams did a better job than others—but rather that such hiccups did not destroy team unity.

One of our Tate's teams (Team Rigel) performed so well that they won the Best Mission Award among the dozen Pathfinder teams that week.

Throughout the week, we had many hiccups and challenges, from a hurried 10 minutes for lunch to a frigid morning for model rocket launches, from squeaky beds at night to 10,000-plus steps during the day, from a few bumps and bruises to a few trials and tears. Despite these moments, the children supported each other's needs and were a joy to be around.

Learning without Fear

Another interesting observation relates to Tate's children's inquisitive nature and pleasant lack of fear of asking questions. Their enthusiasm for science and willingness to ask questions are genuine and refreshing.

This trait first became apparent during a classroom lecture from a Space Camp expert on how astronauts live in space. Approximately 15 Tate's children were present on one side of the classroom, and roughly the same number of students from a public school in Morristown, Tennessee, were present on the other.

This division of the classroom was not intentional, but it did serve as an illustration of Tate's children's inquisitive nature. As the lecture unfolded, the expert listed interesting anecdotes about living in space, such as NASA not allowing bread in space because of microgravity and messy breadcrumbs. Tortillas are the astronaut's carb of choice.

With each fact or anecdote, the hands of the Tate's children would thrust up to ask the expert a follow-up question. The Tate's side of the room looked like an arsenal of rockets in the form of arms jutting straight up and waiting to launch questions. The other side of the room sat passively. Few, if any, hands raised.

The difference was stark.

At first, I was pretty proud, as any parent would be. Our children were engaged, interacting with the experts and seeking answers to their questions.

How do you sleep in space? Can you take pets? Where do you use the bathroom? What about showers?

The litany of questions was almost endless, and the Space Camp expert was not used to handling such inquisitive children. To his credit, he welcomed the questions, but he soon recognized that he had to deploy an alternative strategy, or he might never finish the presentation. He reluctantly triaged the array of inquiries to better manage his time.

At this point, my mood shifted to some sadness as the deafening silence from the other side of the room began to sink in. The excitement for learning and the enthusiasm for questioning were mainly missing—or more likely repressed—with the children from Morristown.

The Tate's children did not fear asking the expert questions. They were excited to learn. Their minds did not sit idle during the presentation, having never switched to some robotic "receive only" mode. Instead, they had shifted their minds into full-throttle interactive mode. Receive. Transmit. Engage. Interact. Learn. Question.

This moment reinforced the gratitude that Lisa and I have for the opportunity to send Grace to Tate's and my sadness that not every child has that same opportunity.

Interest in learning does not appear—or disappear—overnight but rather accumulates over the years. The little things have made a vast difference, from the homerooms of Ms. Riner to Ms. White to Ms. Cross to Ms. Brainard to Ms. McRae and the other remarkable teachers at Tate's.

Esprit de Corps

Finally, one of the great benefits of the Space Camp trip is the shared experience among the teachers, students, and parents. The pride, fellowship, and common loyalty that we have developed through our joint participation in Space Camp has further encouraged Lisa and me that Grace is at the right place for her to grow intellectually, physically, and socially.

Each year, I have enjoyed getting to know the children in Grace's classes and their parents a little bit better as we interact, and the Space Camp trip has been another opportunity to deepen those friendships. These unique events are special.

These overnight trips reaffirm the sense of a shared community working together to bring out the best in our children. Such a community seems uncommon these days as our lives are busy and our backgrounds are diverse.

Our homes may be spread across the Greater Knoxville area, but these Tate's events unify us by splitting a top-bottom bunk, chasing lost backpacks, or sharing a meal. These experiences with fellow parents may seem unimportant, but I have learned they are vitally important.

When I first dropped Grace off for Kindergarten class nearly five years ago, I fondly remember my brief time with fellow parents as we huddled outside Ms. Riner's classroom. Each morning, we spied inside the window to see our children begin their day, and then off to our work days, we would depart with a few brief pleasantries.

Little did I know then that, five years later, we would be going to Space Camp together and watching as our children worked together to launch the Space Shuttle. Even though the mission was simulated, the shared experience was real, and what a wonderful experience it was.

Godspeed Fourth Grade. Godspeed!

Politics: Fact-Checking.
July 14, 2018

The obsession with 'fact-checking' in America today reflects a shallowness of dialogue. The lack of depth in our conversations manifests as mistrust, which leads to the lazy challenge of 'Where did you get your facts?'

Armed with a smartphone and Google, we are empowered like never before to 'outfact' those with whom we disagree. Our political engagement with one another has moved away from the art of persuasion to the combat of fact-pounding. We now prefer rote facts over meaningful values.

If the persuasiveness of our dialogue hinges on the arsenal of our facts, then we are perhaps arguing about the wrong stuff. Consider the disagreements over the viral memes of the blue-gold dress or the more recent laurel-yanny recording.

The dress meme is a picture in which viewers disagree over whether the clothing has a pattern of black and blue stripes or white and gold ones. The Internet exploded in February 2015 over this picture.

The laurel-yanny meme erupted similarly this year on the Internet, sparking heated debates over whether listeners of an audio recording heard the word "laurel" or "yanny."

The dress color or the sound of the recording is the least interesting part of these memes. The more interesting aspect—and where 'fact-checking' becomes irrelevant—is the deeper cause of the 'alternative facts' between differing human perceptions.

As these memes illustrate, fact-checking achieves little.

Ok. The dress is blue. The sound is laurel.

Those facts do little to change the fact that my friend sees the dress as gold or hears Yanny. No matter how often I correct him with the fact that it's blue or laurel, he still sees it—and potentially will always see it—as gold or hears Yanny.

Wouldn't our discussion be better served by moving past this obsession with fact-checking and moving closer to a deeper understanding of one another?

Love or hate him, one has to acknowledge that President Donald Trump's political power is not derived from his unerring command of facts. Fact-checking to discredit Trump has proven to be a quixotic effort.

Yet, the fact-checking industry that has cropped up continues to grow. Newspapers devote whole columns to fact-checkers, and web pages have created a cottage industry around fact-checking. However, the amount of time and effort required for this new industry has done little to minimize Trump's influence.

Why is that?

While I have no intention of being a Trump apologist, the answer lies not in Trump's facts but in his framing of arguments.

If all that was needed to make political decisions were a tallying of facts on one side of the political ledger or the other, then we would only need a calculator to run our governments, not a Congress, a County Commission, or any deliberative body.

The fundamental goal of fact-checking is to show that one side or the other is lying. The danger in that goal is the implied assumption that one side or the other possesses the "right answer."

The fact-checking fallacy assumes that political decisions are based on absolute truths. The reality is that politics is about moral differences that rarely succumb to simple math equations. Neither side has a monopoly on the absolute correct answer.

The deliberation of arguments—and not the calculation of facts—is the strength of our Republic, our State, and our County. We need Senators, Representatives, and Commissioners to debate the paths of our governments, not HAL-9000s, Megatron, or Google bots.

We must move beyond fact-checking and re-engage in the harder work of deliberating. Human endeavors, as the blue dress and laurel recording illustrate, are complex, and mere facts do little to resolve our disagreements about them.

So, next time a disagreement arises on Facebook, rather than reaching for Google to fact-check our opponent into submission, we should try to reach a bit further toward a deeper understanding of our friends, neighbors, and citizens.

Fact-checking is often a waste of time and resources. We would be wise to put our energies where we are more likely to see a return on our investment.

If our friend sees a gold dress and we see a blue one, our facts may differ, and no amount of Googling will change the other person's perception of the world. We should seek a better understanding of our friend rather than checking his facts.

Googling is easy. Understanding is hard.

CONCLUSION

Immersing in the Local

BECOMING A WRITER HAS been a painful process for me. While my formal education has contributed mightily to this process, the growth in self-discipline necessary has been most rewarding. As I have said, I do not like to read, and I do not like to write, but reading and writing are the hard-won skills from the endeavors in this book. The columns in this book represent a tangible starting point in my journey to become a writer, if I can call myself that.

I hope readers will conclude from this collection that writing, as well as reading, is an important skill to develop. I recall my teachers placing me in a developmental reading and writing class in sixth grade. As children, we are not supposed to know that we are "labeled" as slower than other children, but we do know. After the first few grading periods, I elevated myself into a "normal" class. This situation sticks out because I know I did not have an innate talent for reading or writing. It is something that I have had to work at to acquire. I never had a strong desire to develop these skills in my elementary, secondary, or collegiate years. My primary motivation was to get good grades. I had little self-motivation for reading and writing.

My interest in becoming a writer grew after I took the first steps mentioned in the introduction while working in Virginia. The intense reading and writing required for my PhD further nurtured my growth. Finally, my selection as a Community Columnist in 2007 launched my first foray into writing with an impact beyond myself.

The second conclusion I hope readers will draw from this book is the importance of local issues in our daily lives. The book opens with a quote from Marcia Clark and her turn of phrase on the more famous quote, "All politics is local." This latter quote is most often associated with former House Speaker Tip O'Neill. O'Neill cited this phrase as a national officeholder to emphasize the importance of local issues even at the national level. He would admonish House members who would come to Washington DC and forget their home roots.

Clark's new take on O'Neill's well-known adage is also a good reminder that history has a personal side that we should not lose sight of. For those old enough to remember, Clark served as the prosecuting district attorney in the infamous O. J. Simpson murder trial in the mid-1990s. As a public servant doing her duty to serve the citizens of the Los Angeles area, the toll that long and arduous trial took on her personal life was perhaps undeserved (Clark & Carpenter, 1998). Her quote is apropos as a reminder that the smaller individual moments in the larger strokes of history should not be forgotten.

Personal moments generate connections with others, contribute to our sense of self, build lasting memories, and shape our life stories. These moments slip through the cracks of history but serve us best to understand the world around us. Such moments are not as exciting to read as Lincoln's agonizing decisions over the Union's future, Custer's last stand at the Battle of Little Bighorn, FDR's pulling the nation up by our bootstraps, or other monumental moments that have moved history's mountains.

This book stands on molehills rather than mountains. Knox County's mayor, the County Commission, Black Wednesday, and other local issues will fade with time. Few will remember these moments, but this book is my small attempt to capture my window on Knox County history and my perspective on the politics and issues from 2007 to 2008. I hope the reader finds some enrichment from these moments and this collection, as these columns mark the start of my journey as a writer.

As my journey continues, I hope this collection of essays may inspire others to read more, become a writer, and ponder the personal moments of local issues. Georg Christoph Lichtenberg, a German physicist and satirist, once commented, "Writing is an excellent means of awakening in every man the system slumbering within him" (Lichtenberg, 2012). This quote is true for me. I can attest that the slumbering thoughts within me would not have emerged without the discipline of reading and writing to prod them from the depths of my mind.

Acknowledgments

I WANT TO THANK my wife, Lisa, for reading about the News Sentinel opportunity and encouraging me to enter the contest. Lisa is a great "gift giver" as she is continuously looking for gifts for friends and family in her life. When something pops up, she immediately thinks of the fitting person. Such is the case for the Community Columnist contest. She saw this opportunity pop up, and she immediately shared it with me. Lisa has found the perfect gift in this manner countless times, and I am thankful for her encouragement.

I also must thank my daughter Grace. Over the years, she has challenged me to become a better writer, and I have watched her grow and mature as a writer, too. She is much further along at her age than I ever was, and I am proud of her. She and Lisa have had to endure my frenzied discussions when a column idea pops into my head, and they have had to serve as the first draft editors to hear my raw opinions without much filtering and little polishing. They are saints in the world of first-draft editors.

In addition to Lisa and Grace, a long list of friends and colleagues reviewed the many columns over the 12 months. The list includes Paul Crilly, Bob Stelter, Lee Martin, Kenny & Tracy Smith,

Jeremy & Ariaun Loveday, Tim & Lisa Dean, Paul Slay, Molly Slaughter, Stacey Nichols, David Mumpower, Chris Bohleber, Amy White, Kim Cate, Robert Kadunce, Cathy Quist, Chris Austin, Eric Holcombe, Ashok Mishra, and Porter Alexander. I am grateful to each.

The opinions in these columns in no way reflect the views of people on this list. Many individuals disagreed profoundly with me on my opinions. I am thankful for such disagreement and reminded of Proverbs 27:17, "You use steel to sharpen steel, and one friend sharpens another." I have likely left names off this list, and I do apologize. I compiled this list based on emails from 17 years ago, and I may have made a mistake or two. Please forgive omissions. I cannot thank this list of folks enough, as I enjoyed engaging with them each month on the various topics as much as I did writing each column.

Work Cited

Alapo, L. (2008, 03-28-2008). Making schools seem smaller. *Knoxville News Sentinel.*

Bacevich, A. J. (2008). The Right Choice? *The American Conservative.* Retrieved 2008-03-24, from https://www.theamericanconservative.com/the-right-choice/

Barone, M. (2005). Hard America, Soft America: Competition vs. coddling and the battle for the nation's future.

Bents, G. J. (2002). Examining the effects of year-round education: A literature review.

Burger, W. E. (1995). *It is so ordered: A constitution unfolds.* William Morrow & Company.

BurrellesLuce Top 100 List. (2007). Retrieved 07-03-2007 from burrellesluce.com

Clark, M., & Carpenter, T. (1998). *Without a doubt.* Penguin Books.

Cooper, H. (2004). Is the school calendar dated? Education, economics, and the politics of time. In *Summer Learning* (pp. 3-24). Routledge.

Cox, W., & Love, J. (1998). *The best investment a nation ever made: A tribute to the Dwight D. Eisenhower system of interstate and defense highways.* Diane Publishing.

Daniel, K. (2017). *Thinking, fast and slow.*

Daniel, L. (1981). 'What If You Gave A World's Fair And Nobody... https://www.upi.com/Archives/1981/06/04/What-If-You-Gave-A-Worlds-Fair-And-Nobody/1073360475200/

Davis, S. (2007). The Glue Guys. *Sports Illustrated.* Retrieved 2007-02-21, from https://www.si.com/more-sports/2007/02/21/glue-guys

Editors. (2007). Ethics panel should offer nepotism proposal. *Knoxville News Sentinel*.

Ferguson, J. (2007). In D. Page (Ed.).

Fletcher, D. (1996). Illegal parking in spaces reserved for people with disabilities: A review of the research. *Journal of Developmental and Physical Disabilities, 8*, 151-165.

Flory, J. (2007). Park foes allege law violated Midway group says commissioners met privately in '06, . *Knoxville News Sentinel*.

Gates, B. (2005). *Prepared Remarks for National Education Summit on High Schools*. http://www.gatesfoundation.org

Gatto, J. T. (2002). *Dumbing us down: The hidden curriculum of compulsory schooling*. New Society Publishers.

Grafton, S. T. (2020). *Physical Intelligence: The Science of how the Body and the Mind Guide Each Other Through Life*. Pantheon.

Greene, J., & Symonds, W. C. (2006). Bill Gates gets schooled. *Business Week*(3990), 64-70.

http://web.knoxnews.com/pdf/0525budget_travelpay.pdf. (2007).

Humphrey, T. (2007). High points and low points in 2007 session. *Knoxville News Sentinel*.

Humphrey, T. (2008). TN GOP ready for political shake up. *Knoxville News Sentinel*.

Jacobs, D. (2007). TDOT seeks authority to toll. *Knoxville News Sentinel*.

Johnson, G. (2007). Knox County: Another question. *Knoxville News Sentinel*.

Johnson, L. I. (2007). Change would ease scholarship rule. *Knoxville News Sentinel*.

Kohn, A. (2024). Lowering the Temperature on Claims of "Summer Learning Loss". https://www.alfiekohn.org/lowering-temperature-claims-summer-learning-loss/

Kraft, E. (2007). *The TVC's NCO Enhanced Workforce in Science, Technology, Engineering and Mathematics (NEW-STEM) Initiative*. Tennessee Valley Corridor. https://web.archive.org/web/20080516221627/http://www.tennvalleycorridor.org/ventures/new-stem.html

Krauthammer, C. (1999, 1999-01-22). Clinton's One Big Idea. *The Washington Post*. https://www.washingtonpost.com/archive/opinions/19

99/01/22/clintons-one-big-idea/52dab654-cb80-4713-8626-17838f534591/

Law, L. A. (2007). Citizen's Voice: Lowering GPA for lottery doesn't hurt quality. *Knoxville News Sentinel.*

Lehrer, J. (2010). *How we decide.* Houghton Mifflin Harcourt.

Lichtenberg, G. C. (2012). *Georg Christoph Lichtenberg: Philosophical Writings.* State University of New York Press.

McElroy, J. (2007, 10-04-2007). Sunshine law's "two or more" standard is reasonable. *The Upfront Page Blog.* http://blogs.knoxnews.com/knx/editor/2007/10/sunshine_laws_two_or_more_stan.shtml

Research, C. E. (2024). Virginia Tech Shootings Fast Facts. https://www.cnn.com/2013/10/31/us/virginia-tech-shootings-fast-facts/index.html

Rizza, R. (2008, 2008-11-17). Battle plans, how Barack Obama won. *The New Yorker.*

Schelzig, E. (2008). Bredesen, State budget shortfall could reach $800M. *Knoxville News Sentinel.*

Science, C. o., Policy, P., Century, C. o. P. i. t. G. E. o. t. s., & Science, A. A. f. A. (2007). *Rising above the gathering storm: Energizing and employing America for a brighter economic future.* National Academies Press.

Stasavage, D. (2004). Public versus private deliberation in a representative democracy. *Unpublished manuscript, London School of Economics.*

Statement on Assassination of Martin Luther King, Jr., Indianapolis, Indiana, April 4, 1968. (2024). John F. Kennedy Library. https://www.jfklibrary.org/learn/about-jfk/the-kennedy-family/robert-f-kennedy/robert-f-kennedy-speeches/statement-on-assassination-of-martin-luther-king-jr-indianapolis-indiana-april-4-1968

Steenrod, M. (2008, 02-24-2008). Education bar must be raised. *Knoxville News Sentinel.*

Thompson, T. (2004, 09-01-2004). On that Maglev Train to Georgia... *Business Tennessee Magazine.*

Von Hippel, P. T. (2007). What happens to summer learning in year-round schools. Annual meeting of the American sociological association, New York City, NY,

ABOUT THE AUTHOR

David Lon Page holds a Doctorate of Philosophy in Electrical Engineering from the University of Tennessee and is a Research Scientist in computer vision. He is an amateur political junky and has been active in politics, volunteering in campaigns since the age of ten. This book will be his third self-published work, as no reputable publisher wants to take on his writing. Also, no readers seem to care much either, as his work is far from being a "least" seller, much less a "best" seller. As he awaits writing glory, David enjoys wearing his boxers and t-shirts around the house in Knoxville, Tennessee, where his wife, Lisa, and their daughter, Grace, complain that the neighbors are watching. "Dad, stop running around in your underwear!"

www.ingramcontent.com/pod-product-compliance
Lightning Source LLC
Chambersburg PA
CBHW070642030426
42337CB00020B/4123